Reviving the AMERICAN DREAM

Restoring Fairness and Justice to Our Free Market Economy

Square Deal

"No one business or individual or organization
should have an unfair advantage over the other"
President Theodore Roosevelt 1904

RAYMOND J. PARELLO

PAGE PUBLISHING, INC.
New York, NY

First originally published by Page Publishing, Inc. 2017

ISBN 978-1-63568-531-2 (Paperback)
ISBN 978-1-63568-532-9 (Digital)

Printed in the United States of America

CONTENTS

In 1926, Harry Rothman, who went to work at the age of twelve with a pushcart and a dream, purchased a small storefront on East Broadway, and over the next sixty years, through hard work and dedication, Harry created a New York City landmark that endured until his death in 1986, when it looked as though Rothman's may become only a memory.

At the time, Harry's grandson, Kenneth Giddon, was a bond trader in Boston, considering enrollment in Sloan School of Business at MIT and looking forward to a summer trip abroad prior to settling down in further academic pursuits, when his parents called and asked him to forgo his coming trip and help to liquidate the inventory and assets of his grandfather's store. Kenneth agreed and shortly found himself in Manhattan, working to wrap up his grandfather's life work. As he worked toward this end, Kenneth discovered that this was the last thing that he wanted to do. He did not want to see Harry Rothman's legacy become a memory. Kenneth saw true potential in Harry's store and realized that his grandfather's dream had become his dream. After closing the store's doors for a full year, Kenneth launched Rothman's at Union Square as a new version of his grandfather's vision, an upscale discount clothiers that has evolved into much more with great success, enabling Kenneth and his brother Jim, who joined him during his first year of business, to expand their business. The brothers opened a Rothman's in Scarsdale in 2003.

Not too long ago, Rothman's Clothier was hailed by both then-mayor Michael Bloomberg and American Express CEO Kenneth Chenault for its revitalization and maintenance of its local neighborhood. The Giddon brothers' business was simply following the footsteps of innumerable small American businesses that came before. Reflecting its founder's passion and Kenneth Giddon's vision, Rothman's Clothier had become a mainstay and landmark, sparking other positive growth in what was a dilapidated and dying area of town, helping to create a new and vital business and social community, a historic and common positive side effect of successful small businesses everywhere.

In 2008, the bottom dropped out of the economy, and Rothman's, like millions of other small businesses, experienced a couple of rough years, showing losses for the first time in its twenty-two-year history. Giddon, as for the profitability and longevity of his business, was not one to allow a couple of tough years to dissuade him in his mission. Therefore, he confidently approached several major banks, two of which were holding over one-half of a million dollars in deposits for Giddon's business, in order to secure a $500,000 loan for expansion and maintenance during the downturn. His requests were rejected by all these investment giants. Their reasoning: Rothman's Clothier, despite two solid decades of profitability, had recorded marginal losses during the worst economic downturn since the Great Depression. Where were the Giddon brothers to turn?

This question "Where is a small businessperson to turn for investment?" is the central struggle addressed in the following work. The answer is an inescapable and vital element in any attempt to explain the growing elusiveness of the American Dream for all but the wealthiest members of American society.[41]

Chapter One

A Look At The Problem

My colleagues and I have taken the time to write this book because even though we have "made it" in America, our hearts break over the millions of others who have not made it—and will not make it—unless we make positive changes to our economy and the laws governing it. We have watched the fortunes of others, especially young people, *go from promising to depressing* over the past three decades, and we think it's high time to correct the current system. We would hope that this book plays a part in that.

Until economically challenged, *average* Americans are aware of the forces working against their success; they will not demand the necessary changes in our present economic structure. This perpetual lack of awareness will allow those in American society who have vast shares of power and money to continue to determine the fates of those who are less economically privileged, and this, if we are at all honest, can be called oligarchic rule or an artificial aristocracy.

Is this the American Dream? Is this what millions of men and women have fought and died to preserve? We don't think so!

Thus, we are laying out a systematic case for change, which will allow any American who is willing to embrace hard work and honor a fighting chance to do well for themselves and their families in the country that we love and value for its historic principles of equality, opportunity, and freedom.

It's certainly time for the middle class to stop being squashed and the working class to stop being squeezed onto the very edges of our society. Does the American Dream *have* to die? Are we in a new economic reality that prohibits the fulfillment of that dream? And does that new reality, often called the New Normal, have to be permanent?

We say emphatically, "No!"

Before we propose how to revive the American Dream, let us share with you a bit of evidence in case you think that the Dream is still alive, that everything is okay, and that we will soon emerge from some nebulous rough patch of economic capriciousness.

Many, many serious pieces of research and surveys have recently validated that the American Dream is on life support, if not dead already. One article in particular that you should know about is entitled "7 Facts that Show the American Dream is Dead," by Richard Eskow, a former Wall Street executive and consultant.[1]

The article begins by sharing the dismal truth that 59% of Americans believe "the American Dream has become impossible for most to achieve," in a June 2014 survey.[2]

Unfortunately, the facts support this negative perspective.

Perhaps it would be instructive to define the American Dream. The elements listed in Eskow's article are instructive:

---

[1]

[2]

1. a living wage
2. retirement security
3. the opportunity for one's children to get ahead in life[1]

These don't seem like exorbitant aspirations, and they are still quite possible in other countries. However, they are becoming less and less likely in the United States for a host of reasons, many of them systemic in nature. Here are the grim facts about the stagnation of the American economy and the growing inequality that have all but quenched the American Dream for the last thirty years.

- As Eskow and many others have pointed out, the middle class hasn't seen a wage increase in 15 years.[1] *Fifteen years!* As a result, the median household income has fallen since the 2008 financial crisis. Another consequence of this middle-class shrinkage and struggle has been the extreme rarity of single-earner households which, depending on your beliefs about child-rearing and development, could have major implications for the next generation. The point is, even if a woman (or man) wanted to stay home with the children, he or she can't anymore. And what of single-parent households?
- Debt continues to grow, as any solid compilation of data will reveal. The reason is that in light of the wage freeze, middle-class Americans have had to use credit simply to maintain their way of life, certainly in light of skyrocketing costs in education, homes, and health care. Economists now say that we have a "debt-dependent economy."[1]
- Education used to be viewed as the surest path into the middle and upper classes. Today, it is the surest

path to a mountain of crushing debt. Rather than handing economic promise to our children under twenty-five, we are often handing them six-figure debts after they finish their undergraduate degrees. To give you some hard and fast numbers to quantify this scourge, consider that the cost of a college education has risen 500% since 1985, while the overall consumer price index has jumped just 115%. Even the vaunted University of California system, long regarded as a model for affordable public education, now costs a whopping $32,000+ per year to attend. With a median income of $59,000 in the United States, few can afford even one of the more affordable state college degrees in the country.[2]

- In the midst of all this stress, a little time off would be nice, but Americans increasingly cannot afford to take a vacation of any type. *One in four workers takes no time off every year*, leaving 175 million working days of paid vacation unclaimed.[2] Not only can workers not afford a vacation, many have second jobs that they are unable to get time off from to synchronize with their primary occupation's vacation period. Additionally, numerous news reports have documented cases where workers are let go after taking leave for entirely valid reasons, such as the death of a close family member.

- Not only are Americans far less likely to take an extended vacation, they also are increasingly unable to pay the costs associated with regaining their health. This is another area of scandalous price increases that has crushed middle-class Americans. Here are the numbers: Americans have paid 8% more per year for health care since 2007, resulting in an overall jump of 73% since that time. Meanwhile, their wages have declined 8% over that same period.[2] It's more and more true that you had better hope and pray that you won't get sick, because if you do, you could be in debt for years. Even with the advent of the Affordable Care Act, fewer and fewer Americans are going to the doctor because they can't afford health insurance or they are afraid of what a simple physical will reveal— perhaps a serious illness that will require expensive treatment or a pricey prescription?

• The final fact proving the death of the American Dream for most is the former promise of a secure retirement. As has been noted above, many Americans are wrestling debt rather than saving for retirement. In fact, 20% of those nearing the formerly standard retirement age of sixty-five have not saved a penny for their "golden years."[2] And as you might have guessed, many companies are whittling down pensions as well. That means that the prospect of sitting back and living comfortably after a lifetime of praiseworthy hard work is highly doubtful for most Americans now.

Depending on how you define the American Dream, other experts have more hope for its revival, although nearly all of them admit that the situation is dire. The definition given by David Francis of *U.S. News & World Report* in his article "Is the American Dream Dead?" also helps to accurately characterize the elements of traditional aspirations for Americans.[2] He defines it as the United States serving as "the land of opportunity" and that "anyone can achieve success through hard work." For decades, the United States has set the pace for the rest of the world, via the example set by honest capitalism in the linkage of work ethic to prosperity, and we should continue to do so.

Francis goes on to rightly point out that the possibility of achievement through capitalism has been the lure for millions of immigrants throughout our history. In essence, what this book will examine is about even more than our bank accounts and credit scores, our interest rates and foreclosure numbers—it's about what gives our country its essence and character, and part of that has always been the prospect of accomplishment, thanks to putting the nose to the grindstone. In short, America has long been one of few places on the planet where you can become a huge achiever no matter what family name you have, what country your ancestors came from, who you know or don't know, or what your starting point was. That's why our reigning inequality bothers so many of us so much; it strikes at the heart of what America has been. As Francis said, America "has given hope to people born without privilege."[2]

That last phrase is progressively more in peril. Nobel Prize–winning economist Joseph Stiglitz points out that the percentage of income going to the famed 1% of top American wage earners has doubled since 1980, with a three-fold increase to the elite of the elite, the top 0.1%.[2] And this is about more than everyone getting a fair piece of the pie, or at least the opportunity to get a slice large enough to live on. Such drastic inequality, so readily seen in developing countries, could lead to the type of frequent societal and political upheavals that those countries witness. The Organization for Economic Cooperation and Development has warned that "structural income inequality in the United States threatens the long-term strength of the country."[2]

The use of the word *structural* in that analysis highlights another truth: much of our problem is due to structure, not human nature or a lazy generation or "welfare queens" or any other endemic social or behavioral factor. It's a structural problem that can be fixed, as will be explained in later pages.

Some economists would take issue with the use of the word *structural* to describe the problem that's forcing more Americans downward on the economic ladder. Those who disagree with this adjective prefer the term *cyclical* and point to other periods in our history where the economy has rebounded and enabled millions to again ascend. Those optimists are telling everyone to calm down and wait for an inevitable recovery, an economic state where the American Dream is revived and acclaimed again.

Mounds of evidence prove that this is doubtful, as does the experience of the Giddon brothers in their search for investors. Here is a business with a two-decade track record of success, and its proprietors struggle to find the capital that they need to expand and weather the economic downturn. During the intervening years following the reopening of Rothman's and the cataclysm that was the 2008 economic downturn, a structural shift most definitely occurred in the American financial system—a shift with vast and far-reaching ramifications. And as will become abundantly clear, this shift, unfortunately, is not cyclical but structural and elementally unfair.

One of the primary reasons to doubt that our woes are cyclical is the ocean of crippling debt that college graduates— the foundational demographic of our prosperity—are forced to assume and carry for years to come. As Brian Domitrovic, a professor of economic history at Sam Houston State University, says, "When you're talking about college kids with $120,000 in debt, nothing like that has been in the scope before. You're going to spike the impossibility of realizing the Dream if you're saddled with that kind of debt coming out the gate."[3]

The Pew Charitable Trusts have long been known as one of the most reliable sources of quality data in the world. Its recent research into the feasibility of the American Dream, particularly

---

[3]

the likelihood of those on the lowest economic rungs to glide into the middle class, proves insightful. As the Pew people put it in a recent survey report, the American Dream primarily refers to "equal opportunity: the belief that anyone who works hard and plays by the rules can achieve economic success." [4] Sadly, as the Pew findings go on to report, "that rags-to-riches story is more prevalent in Hollywood than in reality. In fact, 43% of Americans raised at the bottom of the income ladder remain stuck there as adults, and 70% never make it to the middle"[4]. Indeed, had Kenneth Giddon been faced with the reality that is our current American economic structure, Rothman's Clothier may well have died with its founder.

Somehow a true and vivid catch-22 has become a large part of economic advancement in the United States today. The Pew study found that college graduates were five times more likely to find some economic success than their counterparts, seeming to reaffirm the notion that a sheepskin is still a proven ticket to upward mobility.[4] However, with college costs soaring, increasing as much as 500% in the last thirty years, fewer and fewer young people will be able to obtain that golden ticket.

Other sociological factors beyond the scope of this study include dual-earner families (recorded to be three times as likely to leave the lower class) and whites (twice as likely as blacks to make that escape).[4] Additionally, even though single-parent households might be seen as a New Normal or a completely acceptable family unit, every piece of available statistical data equates such households with economic misery.

Another way to frame the debate over the lifespan of the American Dream is to determine whether it has become more difficult to improve one's economic status. The answer seems obvious, but some continue to argue that the hopelessness and difficult economic straits, in which millions find themselves, today are simply part of a continuous economic cycle that will correct itself in time.

Jim Tankersley, a reporter for the *Washington Post*, did an excellent job of summarizing the opinions of economists favoring the cyclical theory in a recent article on the topic. Tankersley examined the findings of a blue-ribbon panel of experts anchored by Harvard's Raj Chetty.[5] The team found that when all factors were combined, people today have the same chance to advance from one economic rung to another as their grandparents did. That can be viewed as either good news or bad news. One could suggest that this is, instead of reassuring, disturbing evidence of decades of economic stagnation.

The team discerned that two factors pulled the forces of upward mobility in opposite directions: expanded social programs had helped to pull families up, while inequitable trade agreements and federal tax regulations have diminished hope and prospects for many middle- and working-class workers. This study included data spanning the past fifty years, not simply the recent past. This is an essential consideration when examining the results of this particular study. For example, we must remember that the economic prosperity of the late 1980s and 1990s statistically offset the malaise that is the recent and current economic reality in the United States.

In addition, and notably, Tankersley writes: "The findings also suggest that who your parents are and how much they earn is more consequential for American youths today than ever before. That's because the difference between the bottom and the top of the economic ladder has grown much more stark, but climbing the ladder hasn't gotten any easier."[5]

Mobility scholar Lawrence F. Katz of Harvard University paraphrased the study like this: "What's really changed [are] the consequences of mobility. Because there's so much inequality, people born near the bottom tend to stay near the bottom, and that's much more consequential than it was 50 years ago."[5] It's more consequential than it was in 1965 because the people on the lower rungs have to crane their necks at greater angles to see the wealthy in our country as they slip further and further behind.

Again, the results of this study can either cheer you or discourage you. Most analysts said that they were taken aback by the results, which were compiled by analyzing random earnings reports of Americans. It was widely held that upward economic mobility was indeed more difficult today than in the 1960s. Any rejoicing over these findings must be tempered by the conclusion of the panel itself. Regardless of the relationship of the current situation to its past, economic advancement in this country is grinding along at a snail's pace, especially when compared to other wealthy nations such as Canada and Denmark.[5]

To put this in perspective, consider how a person would react if told that their wages would remain stagnant during the entire span of their fifty-year career. Or ask yourself, would Rothman's Clothier remain in business had they not increased their sales appreciably over the course of several years? When wages and/or business stagnate, the entire economy suffers, leading to a large portion of the population living in a discouraged, if not hopeless, economic frame of mind.

The American Dream is indeed dead for a large share of Americans. Few from the lower rungs edge into even the middle class, and few from the range of median incomes climb into the heights of the wealthiest Americans. The belief is that work and good citizenship will pay off with security and some degree of comfort. Therefore, it could be argued that the American Dream is dead, or at least, barely holding on, in the minds and hearts of large section of America. And this reality can be seen everywhere. It is the reality of millions of American families and individuals. Fewer and fewer of those from lower economic levels edge into the middle class, and even fewer members of the middle class are able to climb to the heights of the wealthy. Incentive is dying, a byproduct of fading hope.

The American Dream may not be dead, but it is certainly in critical condition. Its prognosis remains uncertain. But it could, with wise structural changes, be revived and, indeed, become as robust as it was at its inception.

CHAPTER TWO

THE WELL-DOCUMENTED DIFFICULTIES OF THE MIDDLE CLASS

Regardless of whether or not one believes that economic mobility is more possible than it was in the 1960s, there is one undeniable fact that can be found in nearly every recent study, along with truckloads of anecdotal evidence, and that is the America's middle class is hurting more than ever, despite various well-intentioned, but disappointingly ineffective, government programs designed to cure, or at least medicate, this beleaguered and diminishing demographic.

The current presidential administration has seen the declining population numbers of the American middle class; hence, it seems as if every other day we hear about a government initiative to "help the middle class." These initiatives have limited effect, however, and this book will call for a complete uprising that leads to permanent structural change, not more ineffectual government programs. Yet in case you have any doubt about the veracity of the claim that the middle class is in mortal danger, chew on a few of these numbers.[6]

Instead of more of the same, we must demand a reexamination of the structure of our economy and a targeted reconstruction of certain key elements of its current structure. While doing so, it is imperative to keep all of the following in mind:

- The middle class has declined in percentage of total households from 61% to 55% over the past forty years.
- Median family income dipped by 3% from 2000 to 2015.
- Student loan debt has passed the $1 trillion mark.
- 41% of Americans have medical bill "problems" or are paying off medical debt.
- 1/3 of Americans do not pay their bills on time.
- 2015 income gain distribution in the United States: 34% to the top .01% of the population and another 54% to the top 1%, leaving *12% to the bottom 99%.*
- The United States lost 10% of its working-class jobs between 2000 and 2015 despite a growing population.
- Men between the ages of thirty and fifty saw a 5% decrease in their actual wages between 1980 and 2015 when inflation is figured in.
- One in four American workers makes $13 an hour or less!
- 77% of Americans live paycheck-to-paycheck, at least some of the time, and 18% of these respondents stated that they and/or their family have experienced food insecurity, at least once in a given year (2015).
- One in six seniors lives in poverty.
- And perhaps most distressing for many reasons, the least of which involves the future prospects (educationally, socially, and economically) of these chil-

dren—one of five children struggle in situational and generational poverty in the United States today.

These numbers should appall you, not numb you. It is scandalous that one in five children in the United States lives in poverty and that 3/4 of us have to live paycheck-to-paycheck at times. Obviously, our economic system is broken.

If these numbers shock you or appear unbelievable, you probably need to get out more. When you do, you will notice commonplace examples of struggling American families. They are everywhere. Parents as a coherent unit or single families using SNAP benefits and/or counting products and pennies at the checkout counter, perhaps forced to return something in order to stay on a limited budget, to save a dollar, or because they are simply running shorter than they thought. Take the time to drive around formerly thriving neighborhoods where For Sale, For Rent, and Foreclosed signs abound beside other driveways full of cars, as multiple families share the same residence, with no cultural precedent.

The hard data is overwhelming, as is the anecdotal evidence. The middle class is shrinking and suffering. Every time census figures are released, the news gets worse. Carol Morello of the *Washington Post* wrote a comprehensive round-up of the latest bad news for middle-class America, explaining why the bulk of Americans do not believe the economy is improving, despite any number of positive statistics emanating from Washington.[7]

The 2014 census revealed a growth in inequality of 1.6% in a single year, the greatest hike in almost two decades. Perhaps that is why one-third of Americans see themselves as lower class or lower middle class—they are probably right! As Sarah Burd-Sharps of the Social Science Research Council said, "It explains the disconnect between the numbers saying there's slow improvement and job growth, and the way people feel, because they *haven't* recovered. It's partly because the recovery has mostly been felt at the top."[7]

Tim Smeeding of the Institute for Research on Poverty said of the growing working class (top salary $62,000): "Their pay rate has gone down, the number of hours that everyone in the house works has gone down, their homes have lost value. These are the people really ravaged by the recession."[7]

Those people are not far away. They could live next door to you, sit next to you at church or in the synagogue, or share a wall with your cubicle at work. They are being pulverized by forces far out of their control.

What Jane Waldfogel, a professor at Columbia University's School of Social Work, reports should also bother us all: "What's disconcerting is that inequality is going up post-recession, and it's happening because the top is starting to pull away again."[7] Peter Edelman, author of *So Rich, So Poor: Why It's So Hard to End Poverty in America*, added another somber note: "It's still very, very troubling, it's a very serious picture. We've added 15 million people in poverty since the turn of the century."[7]

It's high time that our potentially great country begins to, once again, increase the population of the upper middle class, instead of increasing the population of the poor and economically devastated. It is time for a structural realignment and an end to rampant, unbridled crony capitalism as the fruition of a revolution wage at the voting box.

It could be argued that the working class of our country has done this to themselves via unionization, skills stagnation, etc. However, quite the contrary is true. The American working class has nothing to merit the difficult circumstances in which it finds itself. American workers have not lost, and are not losing, their traditionally strong work ethic. Instead, American labor is more productive than ever. But rather than being rewarded for their nose-to-the-grindstone, high productivity, the working class is buried further under debt and the monthly bills of simple survival: water, electricity, and shelter. Every other Friday, when they cash or deposit their checks, the money is largely gone. These people, a huge portion of the population, are living in an absurd economic labyrinth, where around each turn they find that their dreams have been replaced by a struggle for survival or a scramble to maintain an elusive status quo. It's like a bad film, in which hard-working people are stuck in a time loop, and from which there is no escape.

The Economic Policy Institute has been a keen observer of this bad movie over the past several years. In one recent issue brief, it shared this conclusion along with several upsetting statistics: "All workers have suffered from decades of stagnating wages despite large gains in productivity."[8] The brief then went on to share these numbers:

- US productivity grew by 62.5% from 1989 to 2010, while wages grew just 12%!
- Almost all the wage growth that American workers enjoyed occurred in the late 1990s, a boom long passed.
- Since 2000, even workers with a college degree have not seen any true wage growth.

The accurate and sobering conclusion of their extensive research made abundantly clear: "The ability of the economy to produce more goods and services has *not* translated into greater compensation for... workers." This increased productivity means profits—profits which are vast and out of all proportion to the stagnant wages the workers who helped to create them, but see themselves overburdened and stuck.

The brief's writers posed several questions that have burned in many hearts for a long time: "Why has pay fared so poorly overall? Why did the richest 1% of Americans receive 56% of all the income growth between 1989 and 2007, before the recession began? Why are corporate profits 22% above their pre-recession level while total corporate sector employees' compensation is 3% below pre-recession levels?"

The brief's authors gave this accurate and inflammatory explanation: "The answers lie in an economy that is designed to work for the well off and not to produce good jobs and improved living standards." This is completely unacceptable by any stretch of morality or long-term viability.

The writers also address government "policies [that] have served to erode the bargaining power of most workers, widen wage inequality, and deplete access to good jobs." It could well be argued that this is by direct design. The elimination of joint and individual bargaining power and, as will be explored further in detail, the elimination of a key aspect of capitalism, competition which has been the hallmarks of governmental economic policy for the last thirty years.

It sounds as if we need new policies. The elements listed in the analysis above combined antithesis of the American Dream. Rather than hard-working people from all walks of life, having strong bargaining power, collective bargaining is being eroded rapidly by laws designed to do just that. Rather than greater access to good jobs, access is rapidly decreasing. And most distressingly, rather than offering equality to all, socioeconomic inequality is reaching an all-time high.

Not long ago, a short, powerful video appeared on YouTube. The piece attempted to present typical American ideals regarding fair income distribution. It was very telling, revealing that many people have little idea about how much today's economic reality differs from optimum economic conditions.[9] The video cited a recent and extensive Harvard University survey, which unsurprisingly showed that nine out of ten Americans think our country's wealth should be distributed equitably, with the top 20% of wage earners gathering a bit over 20% of the wealth available, and the lowest 20% getting a bit under one-fifth of the wealth. That is a bedrock American attitude: those who work hardest and hustle the most are indeed entitled to a bigger share of the pie. And most respondents also believe that even those who have not been fortunate enough to land high-paying positions should get *some* of the pie.

Another piece of the survey, which also should not stun anyone, is that those five thousand people surveyed believed that income distribution was nearly congruent to what the respondents believed was "fair." However, the reality, demonstrated by a vivid, colorful bar graph, shows a microscopic share for the bottom 40% of our country, with the infamous 1% gobbling up nearly one-third of our land's wealth. The graph also reveals that the 1% has more wealth than the majority Americans believed that the top 20% has.[9] The video destroys the myth of equitable wealth distribution in this country. To believe otherwise is to live in an ignorant and dangerous fantasy land.

Further graphic data unveiled in this video depicts the distribution of the $54 trillion of wealth in our nation. The ideal, as voted on by nine of ten Americans, looks like a pile of dollars that steadily, but not markedly, rises as the different sectors of society are considered. There is a fairly sharp upswing at the far right of the graph as the richest people in our country, people like Bill Gates and Steve Ballmer, sit on huge wads of cash. It's doubtful that anyone begrudges those innovators their money, and if the actual distribution looked like the *L* on its back with short legs, many of you would not be feeling pinched on a daily basis!

However, when the *actual* distribution of wealth flutters down like dollars on the fortunate, the graph gets very, very ugly. The far right pile of dollars gained by the wealthiest Americans reaches so high that it doesn't even fit onto the graph. The top 1%'s share of wealth stretches ten times higher than the graph can show, a stunning visual. That is chiefly because that tiny slice of the population owns 40% of our wealth.[9] Their share of income has tripled in the last thirty years, which was the impetus of the Occupy Movement. These folks lived in tents all over the country in a valiant but necessarily transient attempt to draw attention to the growing inequality in the United States.

As the narrator calmly stated, "The poorest Americans don't even register; they're down to pocket change. And the middle class is barely distinguishable from the poor." That's due to the fact that the bottom 80% of Americans own only 7% of our country's wealth.

Perhaps the most poignant question that the narrator poses near the end of this powerful piece will resonate deeply with you: "Do you really think that the CEO is working 380 times harder than his average employee?" We all should be able to agree on an answer to that question: he or she works hard, but not *that* hard!

To put this in a more clear perspective, the average employee needs to work a month to equal what his or her CEO makes in one hour. As the narrator concludes, all we need to do in this country is to wake up to the fact that the reality is not even close to what we think it is.[9] We don't need socialism or some other system of economics. What we need is a level playing field for investment.

The *Mother Jones* website might seem an odd place to find economic analysis, but it did have a powerful article on the stark inequality in our country. Entitled "It's the Inequality, Stupid," the post hits the nail on the head.[10]

The "article" is actually a collection of graphs that tells the same story of the YouTube video mentioned above, also in full and living color. The cruel irony of many of the article's numbers are that they come from 2007 data before the housing market crash, which disproportionately hurt the bottom half of American classes, as those people had much of its wealth tied up in mortgages. Meanwhile, the 1% had just 10% of its wealth tied into housing, making the crisis far more palatable for that group and exacerbating the existing inequality.[10]

The *Mother Jones*'s graphs have all sorts of discouraging, but accurate, titles like "Winners Take All" and "Out of Balance." One very important and notable graphic, titled "Capital Gain," exposes the reasons behind the militant maintenance of the status quo. In addition, it displays the harsh reality and the overwhelming odds against the average American family, with $120,000 in net worth, increasing their financial standing to that of a millionaire. One in twenty-two American families with this solid foundation will achieve this level of success. It is also very telling that the odds of being a millionaire in Congress were just one in two! The House of Representatives alone has five members with a net worth of more than $200 million.[10] With statistics like these, it would seem that the status quo is very safe.

Think of the one group that does not want to change the current rules of the economic game. Who is that? The rich, of course. They have profited wildly from the current system, and they will of course be loath to change any of the laws and regulations that have made them obscenely rich. Well, that includes about half of our congressmen, at least! They are not hearing the cry of the average American because they are getting wealthier every day under current law and economic policy. Of course, they are not going to scream for change or listen to those screaming for change, or even a level playing field.

Another one of these graphs, titled "Who's Winning?" shows that the 2001 Bush tax cuts lowered the tax percentage rate of the ultra-wealthy to levels not seen since the 1930s. Is it at all surprising that the millionaires in Congress would adopt the myth of "job creation" and perpetuate the thirty-year propaganda of trickle-down economics to justify their self-interested votes for such a questionable and inequitable structure. It is simple to quickly calculate how much more these wealthy legislators would have to pay on their millions if that rate were to rise a percentage point or two. Even compared to the era of Ronald Reagan, the latest wave of tax breaks for the 1% is incredible. The 1982 Reagan cut lowered the rate for millionaires to 47.7%; Bush's cuts took it down to 32.4%.[10] No wonder the rich are getting richer!

Coupled with these tax numbers, the *Mother Jones* piece goes on to starkly point out that as the infamous Leona Hemsley used to say, "Only Little People Pay Taxes." This little graphic shows, in living color, a 392% increase in income for four hundred of the wealthiest Americans between 1992 and 2007, while during the same period, these wealthiest of the wealthy have seen a 37% decrease in their tax rate.[10]

Another graphic in the same piece, "You Have Nothing to Lose but Your Gains," illustrates that "if the median household income had kept pace with the economy since 1970, it would now be nearly $92,000, not $50,000."[10] That hurts. Ask the solid middle class if they would appreciate a salary increase to near six figures to match our country's output, and you would hear louder cheers than at a Brazilian World Cup party.

It's one thing to examine statistical evidence that the middle class is being squeezed, downsized, and nudged into the lower class in greater numbers; it's another to examine why this has occurred. Fortunately, abundant articles in recent years have given insight into why this silent killer of the American Dream has spread across our land.

The first reason why inequality has mushroomed while the middle class has sunk lower and lower on the ladder of opportunity is because from the 1970s into the 2000s, the top 20% of American wage earners saw a $2,550-per-year jump in income, while the bottom 20% saw a miniscule rise of just $1,330 *total* during the corresponding decades.[11] That alone has been enough to leave many on a slippery economic ledge, balancing just above the poverty line, while a fortunate few dance merrily into extreme overabundance.

Secondly, the huge income disparity between executives and their labor force, which has reached truly scandalous proportions, has been due not only to miniscule gains in low-income wages but also to the failure of the minimum wage to have any real buying power today. For more information on this, one need only read Barbara Ehrenreich's classic book *Nickel and Dimed* to experience what happened when the author attempted to survive for a full year on the wages of a waitress, a housemaid, and Walmart employee. Ehrenreich was unable to afford minimal rent at a shoddy domicile, let alone support any dependents. The book is a heartbreaking and hard-hitting rebuttal of the idea that the poor are poor because they don't work hard. On the contrary, some of the hardest-working people in our nation live in poverty simply due to the inadequacies and inequities of wages and opportunities in America of the twenty-first century.

In recent years, despite earlier prognostications about a golden era of white-collar job growth, the heaviest upsurge in job opportunities has actually come in low-wage occupations, many of them in the service industry. As those jobs have been produced, wages have been depressed even more ruthlessly as millions of unemployed or underemployed people scramble for the openings.[11]

Add in the generous tax rates afforded to the rich and you get the beginning of the sublime to the ridiculous.

Knowing why is some consolation for the curious who wonder how America ever got to this point; how we went from a country of blue-collar workers rising into the middle class to a nation that has an entrenched elite that gobbles up ever-larger amounts of resources and wealth. Now, the question is: can this be rectified? Can all of this bad news be turned around into good news? Can the United States again be a place where reasonable dreams of success come true? Absolutely, if and only if the investment playing field is once again made level in this country.

One fact is certain: nothing will change in our economy until its structure is altered. As Tankersley, the aforementioned *Washington Post* reporter, related in a recent series on the struggles of the middle class: "In this new reality, a smaller share of Americans enjoy the fruits of an expanding economy. This isn't a fluke of the past few years—*it's woven into the very structure of the economy*"[12]. Tankersley goes on to state that "tax cuts, stimulus spending and rock-bottom interest rates" have not and will not "jolt" the middle class back to its postwar prosperity. No, more is needed. No bandage can cure this. Major structural changes need to be made in the economy.

CHAPTER THREE

THE MIDDLE CLASS IS SHOWN THE CURB— WHAT HAPPENED TO AFFORDABLE HOUSING

The alarming inequality that exists in the United States can seem to be a very distant and invisible problem. We can look at endless charts and graphs, hear from numerous academics, or read lots of angry editorials. But one very, very clear measure of how the middle class is being squeezed and pushed down is a walk through pleasant neighborhoods both within and around our great cities.

What you will discover, in far too many American neighborhoods, is that the middle class has been priced out of them! The sad fact is that the average working American cannot live in any of a given city's neighborhoods unless that quarter is run down or in a northern city that is pounded by difficult weather for more than half the year. America's population has moved to the cities and to the South, leaving vast sections of northern cities vacated and pushing hard-working wage earners to the periphery of the cities in what is now called the exurbs.

The result is that in many parts of the country, the hardest-working among us are compelled to endure incredibly long commutes to work in cities that they can only fantasize about living in. That delivers an evident double whammy to middle class: they pay far higher gas and maintenance costs on their cars or endure longer (and more expensive) mass transit rides than the rich, and anytime they want to take advantage of the cultural and culinary delights of the city, they have to shell out a considerable amount simply to make it into the metropolis.

If you've ever seen any of *The Hunger Games* movies or read the books, you know what a completely bisected society looks like, with the ultra-rich and powerful living in immaculate towns while the poor live in ugly, run-down mean streets many miles away from the alabaster cathedrals of the rich. In *The Hunger Games* and other similar dystopian novels, these two worlds are separated by barbed wire and other barriers and guarded by armed security personnel and twenty-four-hour surveillance. Thankfully, we haven't come to that point yet, but if you don't think that dozens of American cities are unaffordable for the middle class, you haven't done your homework.

There is one society that does closely resemble *The Hunger Games*, a fact validated by satellite photographs, intelligence agencies, and eyewitness testimonies of escapees. That society would be North Korea, where the elite huddle together in Pyongyang, the capital, while the countryside is filled with starving farmers and prison camps. We are a good distance from that sort of segregation, but we are moving steadily in that direction, and this chapter's facts and figures aim to prove this point.

The death of the American Dream does not only mean that a middle class person cannot live in a neighborhood that he or she desired to; it increasingly means that he or she is unable to even buy a house in many metro areas around the country unless, of course, that house is located near a medium-sized northern city watching its population steadily decline due to the lack of real opportunity. It's almost as if a silent civil war is being waged, but this time the South has won decisively.

Many of the studies cited to document the difficulties of the middle class in America were done before the crushing crisis in 2007–8, when millions of homeowners who had been assured by banks and realtors that they could afford the American Dream—a large house with a white picket fence in a quiet suburb—found out that they could not, in fact, make their mortgage payments. The result was a multipronged blow to even those who were able to remain in their homes, sort of like a whip with multiple knots tied on the ends. For one, the value of their homes often plummeted, making it extremely difficult to sell if they needed to move or wanted to get a larger domicile for a growing family, for instance.

Secondly, the purchasing power of Americans seemed to vanish overnight, wounding some businesses and killing others, meaning that hundreds of thousands were suddenly unemployed just because many of their neighbors were allowed to purchase a home that they could no longer afford.

Finally, interest rates nosedived, making it possible for those who grabbed interest-only loans to stay in their homes for a few years longer, but instantly making it foolhardy for people to save. That drag-on interest rates has also hurt IRAs across the country, making retirement a much more perilous financial move for future retirees, who are seeing a minimal return on their pension as the funds they've saved grow at less than a snail's pace.

It is simplistic to trace all of the current recessionary conditions back to the housing crisis of 2007–2008, but it certainly was the primary steamroller to the American Dream for many, and the resulting correction has made home ownership an increasingly rare privilege for the middle class, the final consequence of this body punch to the American Dream.

Now the great debate is similar to the structural-versus-cyclical perspectives regarding the economy at large. Many believe that a recovery in the housing market is inevitable, although it has been interesting to watch estimates for that recovery being pushed back again and again. Others have assembled solid data to argue that the US housing market may never be the same after the Great Correction of '08.

One such perspective was outlined by Karen Weise for Bloomberg in her 2014 story called "Why America's Middle-Class Housing Crunch Is Here to Stay."[13] Weise cited numbers from the respected real estate website Trulia for her argument, summarizing the dire condition of the housing market this way: "Over the past year the housing market has become less affordable in almost every major metro area," adding the dismal fact that in "megaregions" with more than four million in population, "more than half the homes on the market are too expensive for middle class buyers."

Not to get too dramatic, but isn't it enough that the top slice of American wage earners make hundreds of times more than the average American? Do they have to push many of those hard workers out of the housing market too?

Weise relies on the outlook of Jed Kolko, Trulia's chief economist, who wrote that those popular regions will not become more affordable anytime soon. He cited the two-headed problem of stagnant incomes, coupled with long-dormant interest rates that are beginning to creep up—this combination will keep the housing segment of the American Dream just out of the reach of millions of would-be home buyers for the foreseeable future. Additionally, new home construction remains sluggish; thus, the accepted relationship between supply and demand remains at an imbalance for the middle-class family wanting to buy their own place.

This is especially true of many of the more attractive regions of our country, where a middle-class family could only dream of living today. The Trulia study showed that regions where greater supply could help to steady already-high prices were where the fewest new units were being built, historically attractive cities such as San Francisco, Honolulu, New York, Boston, and Miami. As anyone who has visited or gotten a job in Silicon Valley can attest, you probably need a strong six-figure salary to even dream of a tiny abode in that part of the country. The middle class need not even sniff the Bay Area, New York metro region, Boston's suburbs, or the tropical areas of Honolulu or Miami.

Proof of this new, unattractive phenomenon was the startling fact that not a single home on the market in San Francisco recently was affordable on a teacher's salary, according to Trulia.[13]

Obviously, land is limited in popular cities; thus, any new construction will probably have to be vertical and not in the form of individual single-family dwellings. Consequently, if the American Dream could be ramped down to include just a tiny apartment in Miami, then the Dream is still alive for everyone!

Yet even that fairly grim prospect is not likely for many Americans hoping to move to the more desirable areas of our country. The reason is that the people who already live in these alluring regions do not want any more construction near them. It's not as bad as *The Hunger Games*, but it is not far off. The ultra-rich don't want to hear the noise of jackhammers or have their commute home impeded by construction sites.

They have little interest in others getting a sliver of the Dream by living in an attractive region. Besides, if more homes were built, property values would be negatively impacted. The result is extremely limited construction in many metro areas.

Barred from the top-rated American cities, the middle class is moving into so-called midsize cities at such a rapid rate that these burgs are now under strain. Think Austin and Denver, Weise reported. For even those cities to provide housing for the average wage earner, a rise in salary for low- and middle-income workers would be mandatory, but widely reported initiatives to raise the minimum wage, even in progressive cities like Seattle, call for slow increases over several years' time. Weise concludes: "Without housing costs going down or incomes rising in a meaningful way, little relief is in sight."[13] This seems to put to rest the "cyclical" argument.

Not only is the middle class being pushed out of the most highly-sought-after metropolitan areas, but also they are increasingly being shuttled into our country's coldest outposts. In other words, it's not enough that teachers can't buy houses in many cities, but the middle and working classes are almost being forced to shiver rather than sun themselves. As Trey Garrison wrote for the Housingwire.com: "Where it's cold it's affordable; where it's warm you can't buy."[14]

Pointing out that "the most affordable markets are near the Great Lakes," Garrison also reported on data that was analyzed by Trulia's Kolko. Kolko cited grim numbers such as just 15% of homes within the reach of the middle class in San Francisco, with affordability diminishing by the day in warm-weather climes such as Austin and Miami. Another interesting number was Kolko's claim that just more than half of the homes on the market (59%) were within reach of the middle class, down from 62% in 2013.[14] Obviously, the American Dream would have that percentage far closer to 100%, if in fact the Dream was available to all.

Kolko backs up all his remarks with solid mathematical evidence, stating that each metro area's local median household income is calculated, then the percentage of homes on the market that can be purchased with a payment that takes 31% or less of that income each month are tabulated.[14]

Where are the highest percentages of homes that will not bust middle-class budgets located? Hello, Dayton, Rochester, Akron, Gary, and Toledo![14] Nothing against those cities, but they don't quite have the same cache or real or perceived quality of life as Miami or Boston.

The least affordable markets sound more like the types of places where people report high satisfaction-of-living numbers, cities such as San Francisco, San Diego, New York, and Honolulu. Let's be honest: we've become so accustomed to our imbalanced economy that we have never imagined that we could live in Honolulu. That is proof that we have, in fact, become numb to the unjust realities of our economy, which has fenced in Miami while forcing the cramped masses to do their best in Buffalo.

USA Today also reported on this troubling swing in its analysis of the Trulia data. In an article entitled "More Homes Are beyond Reach of Middle Class," Paul Davidson and Meghan Hoyer shared these startling numbers in percentages of affordable homes for the middle class. Note the whopping change in just one year's time!

Least Affordable Housing Markets for the Middle Class

Metro Region	State	Change in Affordable Homes (2013-2014)	Homes Affordable to Middle Class
Ventura County	California	-33%	29%
San Francisco	California	-31%	14%
Orange County	California	-29%	24%
Los Angeles	California	-27%	23%
San Diego	California	-27%	28%
Denver	Colorado	-25%	50%
San Antonio	Texas	-23%	48%
Austin	Texas	-22%	43%
San Jose	California	-20%	34%
Sacramento	California	-20%	50%

[4]cue: 3

One especially disheartening statistic shared in the article was this one: the share of affordable homes decreased in 98 of 100 metro areas between May 2013 and May 2014, with a few cities showing unbelievable dips in percentage of affordable homes—Denver (67% to 50%), San Antonio (62% to 48%).

Erik Sherman of Dailyfinance.com sums up this discouraging phenomenon well in the first paragraph of his recent story "Middle Class Can't Buy Homes in Most Big Cities." He writes: "If the traditional American dream is homeownership—getting the starter, trading up as the family grows—then in most of

---

4

the largest metropolitan areas, the middle class is officially in a nightmare."[5] And the "nightmare" will only get worse, not better. "Housing prices will continue to pull away from incomes," according to Interest.com Managing Editor Mike Sante.[15]

Sherman cited data analysis by Interest.com, which showed that the middle class could only buy a home in fewer than half of America's twenty-five biggest cities. Will the housing market have an inevitable upswing, as many optimistic experts claim? Sante does not think so. "We've recovered about as much as we're going to recover. However, median incomes were only up a little more than 2 percent in the 25 largest cities," he said.[15]

The Interest.com study differed from Trulia's data slightly by comparing home prices from the National Association of Realtors to income figures from the Census Bureau's American Consumer Survey. It figured how much would be needed to afford a 20% down payment, interest, and other city-specific costs. That calculation brought astonishing numbers across Sante's desk, he said. Some people in San Francisco, for instance, pay 70% of their income to housing costs. "I about fell out of my chair [when I realized that]," he said.[15]

Again, the more affordable housing markets read like a who's who of the Rust Belt and Great North: Detroit, Pittsburgh, and Minneapolis. For those who've needed to move into the more desirable areas of the United States due to job changes or simply because they didn't want to live in Erie, the housing squeeze will have a huge effect on their quality of life in the future. As Sante said: "When you start spending 40% or 50% on housing, that's the definition of being house-poor. You're constantly having to say, 'No, I can't do this' or 'No, we can't buy this,' or, 'No, we can't save money for retirement because we don't have money left over.' We're telling people, 'You have to save for your own

_____

5

retirement,' but then housing costs keep going up, so more and more of the income they have winds up having to be devoted to housing."[15]

Sante touches firmly on the sore spot that we know is unjust in our country's current economic climate. The middle class should *not* have to wipe out its retirement savings just to live somewhere south of Pittsburgh. And those that want to live somewhere other than in a declining urban area should have at least some hope for that version of the Dream. As Sante concluded: "The software engineers and investment bankers are making it impossible for the teachers and firefighters to buy homes in these big cities. I wish I could say this is going to get better, but the best I can say is it may not get worse as quickly as it has. But the trend lines are incomes not keeping with home prices."[15]

He and others have called for decisive government action to make the Dream in desirable cities at least a little more possible for the hard-working middle class. Cities and states need to move to provide moderately priced housing in their regions because "you can't count on contractors doing that because they can make so much more money from more expensive houses," Sante concluded.

Until there is a concentrated effort to build more affordable housing for middle-class Americans, another consequence of the housing crunch has been delaying the purchase of a home for millions, and then those who do rent pay higher and higher monthly notes as that market balloons. When one takes a look at the numbers, one can see that perhaps a significant segment of the ultra-rich is comprised of landlords, as rents climb higher and higher, consuming more of the paycheck of Americans every week.

The Population Reference Bureau has been keeping a good eye on this phenomenon and recently reported just how much of a strain monthly rent payments are on many Americans. In a recent article entitled "The Growing Owner/Renter Gap in Affordable Housing in the U.S.," writers Mark Mather and Beth Jarosz give a cogent analysis of the stark reality that many wage earners face when they need to find a place to live.[17]

Taking a look at the number of people with a "high cost burden" for housing (defined as having to pay more than 30% for housing), the latest figures show that owners who have typically had a lower cost burden over the past several decades now have a far easier time paying for housing—yet another proof that the dream of owning a home is quickly slipping out of the grasp of renters, especially young Americans who had assumed they would almost certainly own a home sometime in their lifetime. How can one save enough to buy a home when rent is taking 50% or more of one's income? The answer is that you cannot gather the necessary down payment for a home if that is your economic reality.

For hard and fast numbers, consider this table, showing the percentage of owners and renters who have faced a high cost burden in each given year:

	1999	2007	2011	2015
Owners	22.0	30.6	29.9	29.7
Renters	39.9	49.3	53.4	54.4

What this chart shows is that the many initiatives undertaken to help homeowners—greater tax breaks, lower demand, tamped down interest rates—have allowed the housing cost burdens for them to rise glacially over the past thirteen years.

Meanwhile, there has been a constant and substantial uptick in the number of Americans struggling to simply make rent on, in many cases, substandard housing. Those two contrasting increases have only exacerbated the gap between home-owners sweating out monthly payments and renters. In 1999, the gap between these two groups was just 18%. Today it is 25% and growing.[17]

The reason for these distressing numbers, according to Mather and Jarosz, are manifold:

- declines in home ownership, especially among young adults
- changing economic circumstances of homeowners versus renters (think rich getting richer)
- recent increases in rental costs

Renters are falling into poverty at greater and greater rates; meanwhile, their rents are increasing as former (and potential) homeowners flood into the rental market, driving up monthly rates. Even though the working class did not attempt to buy homes under the auspices of questionable loans offered by greedy banks, they are suffering the ancillary consequences of the lower middle class trying to acquire a home before it could afford one, the crux of the housing crisis nearly a decade ago.

Other takeaways from the figures provided by the US Census Bureau's American Community Survey were that the profile of homeowners continues to evolve into an older person who has worked for decades to save for a down payment and own a home. The younger generation is less and less likely to even attempt home ownership, and many would not qualify even if they did try. Additionally, many of those Americans who had their homes foreclosed upon in 2007–2008 were younger Americans, hundreds of thousands of young couples jumping at the chance to grab a piece of the Dream only to have the bank snatch it back within a year or two.[17]

All these trends show that the Dream is increasingly distant for the next generation, a fact that should distress anyone who assumed that their children would fare better than they, another long-time American assumption that is going the way of AMC Motors and floppy discs. The Dream is dying not just because homeownership is becoming increasingly harder to attain (and almost impossible to touch in cities with a high quality of life), but also because the traditional engine of our economy—small businesses, lacking the power to borrow or secure investments—has been running out of steam. That has led to massive layoffs and bursting unemployment rolls, leaving millions of Americans, young and old, scrambling to find work at even low-paying positions. It's just another way that the middle class is eroding and wage inequality stretches to more extreme ends of the wealth spectrum.

CHAPTER FOUR

THE LITTLE ENGINE THAT COULDN'T ANYMORE— SMALL BUSINESSES TUMBLE OFF A CLIFF

You've probably heard the saying before: small businesses are the engine of the American economy, or its backbone, or its foundation. Whatever metaphor is used, statistical data can back up the fact that small businesses do indeed help to power the American economy. They create jobs instantly, they help to elevate owners from the middle to upper middle class and beyond, and they are a clear sign of the vibrancy of any economy. And as can be seen with Kenneth Giddon's resurrection of Rothman's Clothier, they rejuvenate economically depressed neighborhoods.

Another glaring proof of the need to take positive action to fix our economy and give more people reasons for hope is the desperate state of the small business owner today. To put it simply: fewer and fewer men and women are taking a chance at starting a small business, an ominous sign, and more and more of them are closing up shop early. Return the key element of capitalism, competition, to its proper place in our economic structure, and this will reverse itself.

A related statistical category that proves further economic malaise is the number of people who are not working in the United States, and the quantity of those who are no longer even looking for work, a true sign of utter discouragement. The federal government can publish as many heartening statistics as it would like, but there are often at least two or three other statistical measures that indicate the American worker is struggling mightily even if he or she wants to work. This is not entirely the fault of businesses that downsize to increase profit, as outsourcing and greater technology eliminate thousands of jobs.

Small business owners also have an array of adversaries in their quest to make a living and employ others while doing so, as can be seen firsthand through the Giddons' experience during their search for maintenance and expansion investment.

Take a look at some of the numbers and what expert analysts are saying about those numbers, and it will quickly become undeniable and undebatable that yet another factor has played a huge role in the middle class getting squeezed and the working class remaining at the bottom of the heap in our country: small businesses are struggling as never before, which means fewer opportunities to create a thriving enterprise that allows upward economic mobility. In addition, a declining number of small companies are healthy enough to hire a steady (or growing) workforce.

Brad Plumer had an interesting take on the state of American businesses in a recent article for the *Washington Post*. In his article "Three Reasons the U.S. Labor Force Keeps Shrinking," Plumer begins with a disappointing number that calls to mind the economic quicksand in which our country was mired during the late 1970s. Plumer noted that just 63.2%

of Americans had a job or were actively seeking work in 2013, the lowest share since the gloomy days of 1978. As of the end of 2015, this percentage has declined to 62.4%. That is close to 3 million people that have given up, thrown in the towel in the employment struggle in less than two years. What adds to the impact of this number is the direction of a graph that was also included in the article (pictured below). The line indicating the percentage of Americans working or seeking a job looks like a waterfall, dipping nearly 5% in the past decade or so. What's worse is that this dip is faster than demographers predicted, as they based their prophecies primarily on the rate of aging in America's workforce.[19]

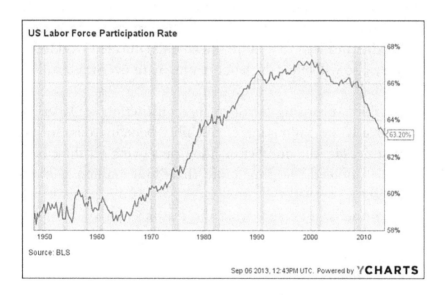

How can this be, with the unemployment rate sinking to its lowest level in five years? Simple. Hundreds of thousands of Americans are simply dropping out of the job market, believing that they are too old, too infirm, or just too unlucky or under-qualified to continue to seek work or keep it. Large numbers of

Americans are retiring, another significant slice is going back to school (often because they cannot find work or believe they need an advanced degree to compete; most of these students will graduate with large amounts of added debt), and others are simply tired of looking for a job that will "fulfill" them.[6]

Baby boomers have retired in droves since 2000, leading to a steadily smaller labor force, and that trend is predicted to continue into the next decade. This was the first of the three reasons cited for the shrinkage of America's work force in Plumer's article.[19]

The second was the return to school of millions of Americans, convinced that they need an advanced degree to become more attractive to employers and not finding what they sought as they applied for jobs and even worked for a time. Again, these millions of students will certainly gain greater knowledge and lead to a more skilled and educated workforce, but they also will enter the labor market with oversized student loan bills.[19]

A third surprising factor in the constriction of America's workforce is the ballooning of disability benefits rolls. In just the past decade, the number of Americans living off these benefits has doubled, keeping more than four million workers sidelined.[19]

No one is quite sure what the reason is for these higher numbers, but there is some evidence that suggests that discouraged workers do look harder for loopholes to receive disability insurance than those who love their jobs and are eager to return to them. A recent *60 Minutes* report uncovered widespread fraud in one Appalachian county, indicating that workers who face job cuts and are unskilled have flocked to lawyers who can

---

6

get them disability benefits through a variety of barely legal tactics.[20]

What troubles analysts the most about the workforce shrinkage is the evidence that millions of workers are simply giving up, which would have a negative long-term impact on our country's productivity—and doom those people to a lifetime of perpetual economic struggle. As Plumer wrote, "If discouraged workers are dropping out of the labor force entirely, they may never make their way back into employment—they may become unemployable. That's a massive human tragedy. It could also mean the U.S. economy will be significantly weaker in the future as a capitalist society."[19]

This proclivity of discouraged Americans dropping out of the job market has drawn increasing coverage over the past year or so, with some analysts rightly pointing out that it's not just older Americans who stop looking for work. A fair number of young potential wage earners have stopped looking for jobs.

As Neil Irwin of the *New York Times* noted in his column "Good News on Jobs: Why Aren't We Happier?" we do indeed have as many jobs available for workers as we did before the 2007–2008 crisis, but we've also added 15 million potential American workers in that time as well.[21] The further bad news, as noted in figures released by the Organization for Economic Cooperation and Development, was that the average private sector worker in the United States made only $20 more per week in 2014 as he or she did in 2008. Of course, the cost of living has far outstripped that very modest pay increase. Meanwhile, the ultra-rich continue to accumulate wealth.

As for discouraged workers, the older set of Americans who have stopped looking for work will probably not get back into the job force. As Irwin asks, "How many of the sixty-one-year-olds who gave up looking for a job in the last few years are going to return to the labor force when they smell opportunity, and how many have retired for good?"[21]

Other commentators dug even deeper into the OECD numbers and found that not only was the senior set choosing to exit the workforce, but "prime age" workers as well. The Center for Economic Policy and Research added as a further note to Irwin's column that the employment-to-population ratio for workers between the ages of twenty-five and fifty-four was down 3.5% from its prerecession level, while for workers aged fifty-five to sixty-four, it was only down 0.9%.

As the OECR succinctly put it, the real question is: why are forty-one-year-olds leaving the labor market? No one is quite sure. As the article's writers stated, "It is difficult to envision any obvious reason why people in their prime working years would suddenly decide that they did not want to work other than the weakness of the labor market."[22]

Forty-somethings and sixty-somethings aren't the only people discouraged by the current economic condition of the United States. Small business owners are taking a bigger risk than ever by attempting start-ups and seeing if their idea for providing a good or service will fly or crash. Numerous recent articles have documented the shocking and sad fact that more businesses close than open every month in the United States. Think of small businesses as having a negative birth rate, which of course means that if the trend continues indefinitely, it could lead to the very death of this pillar in the American economy.

As J. D. Harrison plainly stated in his lead to the article "More Businesses Are Closing than Starting: Can Congress Help Turn That Around?" "Americans are starting fewer businesses, new companies are going out of business more quickly, and the new firms that do get off the ground are creating fewer jobs." And as he added, "None of that bodes very well for an economy still trying to find its footing."[23]

Representatives of organizations that help small businesses have grown concerned enough about the climate for newborn companies that they have begun to appeal to Congress for more business-friendly laws. John Dearie, executive vice president of the Financial Services Forum, a trade organization in Washington, DC, recently testified before members of the House Small Business Committee that all vital signs for those who desire to inaugurate start-ups "are flashing red alert." He buttressed this statement by pointing out that new businesses, which hire a disproportionate number of new workers than any other type of small business, have seen a 40% drop in hiring since 2000. That is partly due to the drop in number of new businesses among all small businesses, a number that has been cut in half, from 15% to 8%, in the past three decades. Additionally, the number of infant firms going under within their first few years has grown dramatically as well. The end result is a negative birth rate for the first time in thirty years, according to the US Census Bureau.[23]

Among the steps sought by patrons of entrepreneurs are the following:

- An overhaul of the immigration system. Entrepreneurs report that a severe shortage of qualified talent continues to crimp their efforts. The most radical idea has called for permanent residency cards for all foreign-born students who have degrees in science, technology, engineering, or math from a US university. Additionally, entrepreneurs from abroad should be granted start-up visas because they start more companies than native-born Americans and are more innovative.

- Reduce student debt. This would free up more people in prime entrepreneurial years (ages thirty to fifty) to start businesses.
- Take down regulatory barriers and simplify and modify the tax code for start-up owners.[23]

Wynton Hill at Breitbart.com was one of many analysts to chime in on the latest figures documenting the difficulties of small business owners when Gallup CEO and chairman Jim Clifton issued a report in 2015 on the state of start-ups in America. Clifton proclaimed, "For the first time in 35 years, American business deaths now outnumber business births."[24]

This negative birth rate has created, according to Clifton, "an underground earthquake," adding, "Let's get one thing clear: This economy is never truly coming back unless we reverse the birth and death trends of American businesses."[24]

Clifton went on to take issue with the figures commonly bandied about when economists talk about small businesses in America. He claimed that 20 million of the 26 million small businesses often cited in labor statistics are actually shams—companies that exist solely on paper with no workers, profits, customers, or sales. Only 6 million businesses have one or more employees, he said, and 3.8 million of those have four or fewer workers. Yet, somehow, these small businesses provide jobs for a whopping 100 million Americans, a stunning testament to their importance.[24]

Thus, a negative birth rate in business is actually far graver than previously thought. If only a fraction of the small businesses listed on paper actually exist and an even smaller fraction employs more than five people, any subtraction from that smaller number will be critical. As Clifton concluded, "I don't want to sound like a doomsayer, but when small and medium-sized businesses are dying faster than they're being born, so is free enterprise. And when free enterprise dies, America dies with it."[24]

Consider the dismal charts and numbers presented by the US Bureau of Labor Statistics (BLS). The number of business establishments that are less than a year old follows a line that looks as if it is dropping off a cliff (see chart 1 below). So many Americans were hit hard by the 2007 mortgage crisis that far fewer had enough capital to launch a business or have access to capital that someone else had. The result was a steep drop in the number of new businesses from 2007 on, with no recovery in sight. As has been stated before, new businesses produce new jobs instantly, many of them at a level accessible by less educated Americans. Fewer new businesses equals fewer promising job opportunities, which translates into millions simply dropping out of the job market. It is simple mathematics and human nature.

The number of jobs created by establishments less than one year old has decreased from 4.1 million in 1994, when tracking of this type of business began, to 2.5 million in 2010. This trend, combined with that of fewer new establishments overall, indicates that the number of new jobs in all types of small businesses is declining.

Chart 1. Number of Establishments Less than One Year Old, March 1994–March 2010

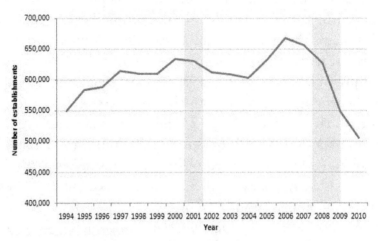

Source: US Bureau of Labor Statistic[25]

Indeed, the correspondence between new business creation and job creation can be clearly seen in chart 2 below. We cannot take consolation in the possibility that the fewer new businesses being created are in fact larger enterprises and thus are supporting more workers. They are not. New jobs spawned by rookie enterprises have also taken a sharp slide.

Chart 2. Jobs Created by Establishments Less than One Year Old, March 1994–March 2010

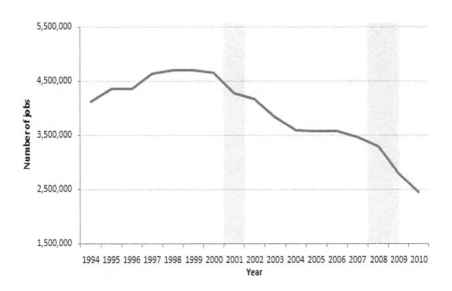

Source: US Bureau of Labor Statistic[25]

Once we see the dipping survival rate for new businesses in recent years, we can understand why fewer entrepreneurs have been willing to launch out and found new enterprises (see chart 3). Yet another economic indicator shows the weakness of the American economy. Look at the light-blue, lavender, and spring-green lines in chart 3 below. You will see that they have the starkest drops—meaning, businesses that begun post-2007 crisis have failed more quickly than those founded in the previous couple of decades. Failed businesses mean lost jobs, as well as workers unsure if they want to believe in the prospect of long-term employment.

Chart 3. Survival Rates of Establishments by Year Started and Number of Years since Starting, 1994-2010

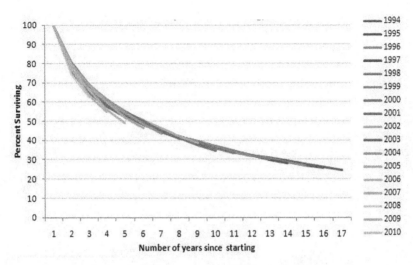

Source: US Bureau of Labor Statistic

Finally, we can see the critical period when business deaths began to outnumber business births. The figures used in chart 5 below are "the most timely source of data available on new private sector business establishments," so it is perhaps the most accurate graph in this chapter. As the BLS noted: "Since the most recent recession began in December 2007, births have experienced the steepest decline in the history of the series. New establishments are not being formed at the same levels seen before the economic downturn began, and the number is much lower than it was during the 2001 recession."[25]

Chart 5. Quarterly establishment births and deaths, 1993-2010

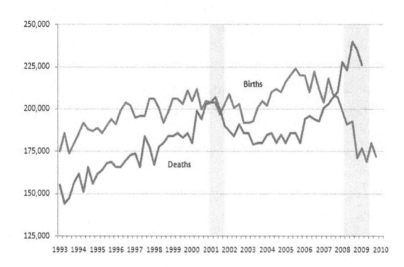

If you see a small business owner, give him or her a hug. He or she will need it. Something is critically wrong with our economy and with our society when bravery and risk are discouraged and where the desire to provide a needed good or service is snuffed out. Every number gathered in the past couple of decades show that starting a small business is more dangerous than ever, and that's why fewer and fewer people are taking that leap.

As these and other businesses fail, workers are downsized quickly and heartlessly. Many of those laid off give up looking for work altogether. Millions of others are scrambling desperately to get a piece of the disability benefits pie rather than continue to seek a job. That's the sign of a truly sick system. Can we blame such people? Perhaps they have been knocked around enough by the capricious job market that they believe in their hearts they are entitled to disability, perhaps for mental suffering?

The federal tax regulations restricting the availability of investment capital for small business, the engine of economic security for the middle class, has caused Americans to increasingly abstain from employment, forego risk to open new enterprises, and hunker down in hopes of just holding on to what they have. Few dream anymore of rising into higher classes—that aspiration has been extinguished by our system—while a chosen few gobble up more and more of our resources and wealth.

Disability benefits fraud isn't the only monkey business going on in our nation. Let's take a look at some of the more bizarre laws of which you may not be aware, but which have a sizeable impact on the state of our economy. Corporate law needs an overhaul if we are to regain our status as a nation that can offer dreams to its people.

CHAPTER FIVE

LEGAL ISSUES WHEN CORPORATIONS ARE TREATED LIKE PEOPLE

Any time you are in a country or society that does not seem to work, you need to ask yourself the question: whose interest is served by the status quo? In other words, who is content to allow a dysfunctional system to continue? The answer, inevitably, is: those who benefit from the breakdown of said system, and in almost every case, these would be the wealthy.

Consider the facts that have been laid out thus far in this book:

1. The middle class is being smashed down into the lower class.
2. The average American cannot afford to live in a temperate, economically booming city.
3. Small businesses are failing at ever-higher rates.
4. The 10% owns an 80% share of our country's wealth.
5. the 10% consume 55% of our country's income

It should, at this point, be clear that the 10% is quite content to keep the American Dream out of the reach of the average worker. This small group of crony capitalists and their fortunate offspring, enjoying their financial and physical security from the hidden luxury of their gated enclaves and compounds, do not believe that anything is wrong with the broken pieces of our current economy. Quite the contrary, the current New Normal serves them very well, "Thank you very much, and there is absolutely no need to change anything."

"Surely," we say, "our elected officials will rein in the runaway Wall Street Monopoly that seems to be rewarded in our nation. Surely they will tinker with the economy so that the American Dream can enjoy a revival."

Ah, but therein lies the problem. For starters, more and more of our elected officials are entering or coming from the corporate market system. In addition, our laws have quietly been altered over many years so that the very people manning the controls, the American corporate market system, have the most to gain by maintaining this distorted competition-free economic system. They are, in fact, pulling and pushing all the levers in today's society while all three branches of government turn a blind eye—because many of those occupying positions of power in all three branches of the government reached their current status thanks to the support of the corporate market system and crony capitalism!

Before you claim that this is an exaggeration or overly dramatic, consider a few of the Supreme Court's recent legal decisions that have helped maintain a system in which the aristocrats truly do call all the shots. There have been several, but perhaps the most obvious is the landmark 2010 decision in the *Citizens United* v. *Federal Election Commission* case, in which the court overturned the ban on certain corporate donations to candidates, ruling that corporations have the same rights as a US citizen. But, if we acknowledge that 15% of our corporate stockholders are foreign citizens, and that the US dollar is fungible, are we not therefore accepting the intervention of foreigners into our political discourse?

A few lone wolf politicians are courageous enough to cry out when they notice a monstrous flaw in the current relationship between business and politics. Representative Adam Schiff (D-California) recently wrote a scathing article for *The Atlantic*, summarizing a 2012 decision by the court that struck down a centuries-old Montana law and extended the Citizens United ruling to state and local elections. In his article titled "The Supreme Court Still Thinks Corporations Are People," Schiff cries foul that, rather than reversing its highly controversial decision, the court instead reaffirmed "that corporations are people—at least as far as the First Amendment is concerned."[27]

In the 2010 decision, the court took the first step down a dark corridor by ruling that the First Amendment prohibited the government from restricting "independent political expenditures" from nonprofit corporations. Since that decision, every entity from labor unions to for-profit businesses have jumped on the bandwagon and funneled dollars to politicians eager to do their bidding. The 2012 decision regarding Montana simply reaffirmed the right of corporations of all types to shower pliant elected officials with money just in case those officials got any ideas about changing the way things run in our economy and society.

Think about it: just how different is the United States from a banana republic if wealthy businesspeople and politicians continually sleep in the same bed? You know the answer to that question.

The Supreme Court did not see it that way. Rather, it declared in its decision: "We now conclude that independent expenditures, including those made by corporations, do not give rise to corruption or the appearance of corruption." What? And it gets worse: "The appearance of influence or access, furthermore, will not cause the electorate to lose faith in our democracy."[27]

The naivety or intentional intellectual negligence of these words boggles the mind, and one can only imagine the rejoicing and celebration to be found in corporate boardrooms when the court expressed such biased and nonsensical ideas in support of corporate market system. The decision sparked a literal stampede, an avalanche of corporate campaign contributions. Such "independent expenditures" have soared into the billions within just a few years. And the word *independent* is a true misnomer as well, as if there is some sort of separation from the office holders and the corporations who want to influence them. Super PACS have gone on to have an influence far beyond what any fair-minded American would desire in House, Senate, and presidential elections. No wonder the average American is so cynical about politics!

Schiff was so alarmed by the Montana decision that he introduced H. J. Res. 111 to alter the Constitution, a proposal created by Harvard law professor Laurence H. Tribe, which stated that "nothing in this Constitution shall be construed to forbid Congress or the states from imposing content-neutral limitations on private campaign contributions or independent political campaign expenditures." Schiff embarked on this quixotic quest to change the Constitution because he believes "this Court has dug in—no amount of unrestrained spending, no appearance of impropriety, or actual corruption of our system is likely to dislodge this newly entrenched precedent from the threat it poses to our democracy."[27]

Strong words, indeed, and a development with which we should all be concerned.

As Schiff stated in his article, "The tidal wave of independent expenditures creates an unmistakable appearance of impropriety, and over time, it cannot help but corrupt.... Corporations are not people."[27]

The very idea that corporations are people has a murky and shaky legal history for an idea that now seems so well established. Most legal scholars trace it back to the 1886 *Santa Clara County v. Southern Pacific Railroad* decision handed down by Supreme Court when Chief Justice Morrison Waite made an offhand remark about the court, agreeing that corporations were to have "the equal protection of the laws."[28] The story gets even more bizarre. A court reporter simply included Waite's remark in the headnotes, and it became an "instant landmark ruling."[28] Little did Waite and the reporter know that more than a century later, this side remark and its notation would be used to open the floodgates of massive corporate influence on our election process and reinforce oppressive crony capitalism.

Tom Philpott of *Mother Jones* makes the cogent point that banks have been one of the leading beneficiaries of the idea that a corporation is a person, pointing to the 50+% share of US financial assets that they currently enjoy, compared to the mere 20% that they controlled in 1990.[29] Is it any wonder that these banks were rescued by the federal government, given their massive investment in political lobbying, an effort that has been accelerated by their perpetually expanding profits? Perhaps if we put *banks* in place of *corporations*, we would all be more up in arms about the idea that businesses are to be treated like people.

Philpott goes on to further examine the harm done by the corporations-as-people reality as he delves into the widely reported death of the once-lauded and most cherished and American of enterprises, the small farm. Philpott demonstrates conclusively that Big Food has far too tight of a grip on public policy in our country, with yet another middle class icon—the farmer—getting crushed under the wheels of "progress."

When influence and control become concentrated in a few hands (a consistent problem in modern America), the major players gain "market power," which enables them to control prices, working conditions, and even processes to an unjust degree. That's why the number of hog farms in the United States, for instance, has plummeted from 240,000 to just 60,000 between 1992 and 2007, and why workers in the food industry have seen their real wages plunge.[29] As a result, the basic and essential human function of feeding oneself is drastically and negatively impacted by "corporate personhood," giving food industry monopolies the unchecked freedom to ply politicians with huge stacks of cash to maintain the status quo and eliminate their competition.

Further, these Big Food monopolies affect the lives of billions beyond the borders of the United States as they establish prices for necessities such as wheat and rice. As food prices have edged up over the past decade, it has not been the American family farmer who has benefited. Instead, about four Goliath agribusinesses have enjoyed record profits. These rising prices prompted the United Nations to state, just recently, that global food prices are far beyond what supply and demand factors should have established as fair.[29]

Perhaps when more Americans begin to grow hungry will we see the sort of outcry that we should over this issue. It is certain that, until there is a deafening roar from millions of hungry US citizens, our elected officials will do nothing. They are far too busy bathing in the showers of cash poured into their campaigns by Big Food.

Philpott wrote that "the political system is so shot through with finance sector cash that it's incapable of properly regulating Wall Street's food fetish." He proved this bold statement by pointing out that agribusiness rained $1.4 billion on lobbying efforts between 1998 and 2011, more than defense contractors and other well-known influence buyers, a dramatic increase indicated in the graph below.[29]

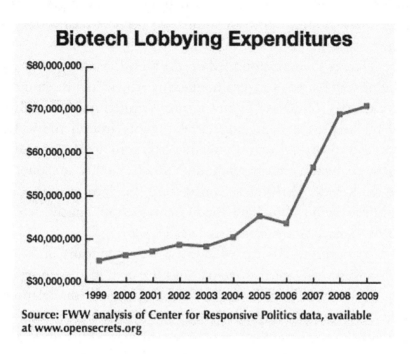

Biotech Lobbying Expenditures

Source: FWW analysis of Center for Responsive Politics data, available at www.opensecrets.org

Actually, we may not even need to go hungry. Perhaps we'll get more upset when we get sick. That could be just around the corner, as more than one-third of USDA and FDA inspectors agreed in a recent survey that "public health has been harmed by agency practices that defer to business interests." More chillingly, 16% said that they "witnessed officials selectively or incompletely using data to justify a specific regulatory outcome" and 10% said that "agency decision makers inappropriately asked them to exclude or alter information or conclusions in an agency scientific document." One USDA veterinarian went so far as to say, "Not only is there lack of support, but there's outright obstruction, retaliation and abuse of power."[29]

Philpott's gloomy conclusion read: "What we're left with is a system of government oversight crumbling in the face of industry influence."[7] Score yet more points for the largest of the large as wealth and power continue to become more concentrated in the hands of a few.

The Economist expounded on the world's view of this cozy relationship between government and business in a recent article entitled "The New Age of Crony Capitalism." The editorial tracked the encouraging developments around the world demonstrating that corruption and backroom deals are becoming passé, while transparency and accountability are on the rise worldwide. One line summed it up this way: even though "political connections have made many people hugely rich in recent years... crony capitalism may be waning."[30]

In an unusual turn of events, we Americans and our own government need to watch and learn from the uprisings around the world that have demanded change in the relationship between political leaders and wealthy businesspeople that the job of government is not to always facilitate big business to grow even bigger, but to ensure that such businesses do not go unregulated to the point of exploiting a country's citizens.

Perhaps Americans can learn a thing or two from their foreign brethren who cried "Foul!" loudly enough inside and outside of Ukraine to lead to the collapse of the regime of Viktor Yanukovych, a man noted for his inner circle of oligarchs, or those in India who voted in a man, Narendra Modri, committed to fighting corruption who rode that platform to victory (to the chagrin of many of the elite in that rising power). Perhaps our press needs to dig around and report a bit better on crony

---

7

capitalism, as sources broke the story of Turkish Prime Minister Recep Erdoğan's illicit deals with construction firms (in a country renowned for lack of press freedom), and perhaps our leaders could follow the example of Chinese President Xi Jinping, who said he would act "without mercy" to root out corruption as he responded to overwhelming public anger and promptly punished 182,000 officials for ethical lapses.[31]

As the editorial happily reported: "As in America at the turn of the 20th century, a new middle class is flexing its muscles, this time on a global scale. People want politicians who don't line their pockets, and tycoons who compete without favours. A revolution to save capitalism from the capitalists is under way."[31]

It's time to turn the clock back and reform our system the way it was overhauled at the dawn of the twentieth century, when robber barons were prosecuted and antitrust laws disassembled monopolies. Consequently, the flow of bribes to US senators slowed to a trickle.

Phenomena that have characterized the latest outbreak of crony capitalism in developing countries, according to *The Economist* and other sources, include mushrooming property prices that have enriched developers who seem to have their projects easily rubber-stamped, no matter what the impact will be on the environment or middle class, and the commodities boom, which has falsely inflated the value of oilfields and mines, thus immediately enriching tycoons who benefit from sudden privatizations.[31]

Before we shake a finger at the emerging world, as we are so prone to do, we need to take a look in the mirror and ask if these two trends are threatening our economy and sense of fairness as well. Indeed, they are; crony capitalism is not restricted to non-Western countries.

The global outcry over the lack of justice in capitalism run amok is not only to restore moral order in world economies—it's good business. As any in-depth studies of nations where crony capitalism has prevailed show, it leads to crumbling infrastructure as firms cozy with the pols know they can do mediocre work, cut corners, and still secure the contract—for perpetuity. By the way, has anyone checked the condition of our roads and bridges lately?

The corporate market system has repressed competition, a key element in American capitalism up until the past few decades, as Main Street investors are squashed by a tax code that unfairly favors Wall Street corporations with long-standing relationships connected to semipermanent leaders. Furthermore, those businesses privileged to have the ears (and hands) of politicians because of their huge contributions help to set a skewed moral tone that demands that the supported politician consider the issues of their supporters. If the leaders at the top are so easily influenced, why shouldn't those on the state and local level be as well?

The three biggest culprits that are almost invariably directly linked to inappropriate government influence—the fossil fuel, banking, and casino industries—all produce an inordinate number of billionaires across the globe. Fortunately in the States, we do not have too many mining magnates or casino kings, but don't think for an instant that the gargantuan banks were bailed out nearly a decade ago solely because our economists believed it was best for our economy. The rescue of those too-big-to-fail banks by unwitting taxpayers involved a dramatic transfer of wealth to certain financiers, while others were led off a cliff. Who made the criteria for deciding who won and who lost? Too big to fail? Indeed! Perhaps "too connected to fail" would have been more apropos.

As we watch the developing world wise up and realize that moral economic policy is sound economic policy, perhaps we can take a page from Brazil, Hong Kong and India, which have all increased the number and power of their antitrust regulators. Perhaps we can applaud and imitate Mexico President Enrique Peña Nieto, who has taken on the telecom and media cartels in his country. We also can watch China sort through its state-owned mini kingdoms and make sure that we have none.[31]

Most of all, we the people need to remember that we do *not* have to remain silent. In fact, if it gets bad enough, we need to make our voices heard. And yes, it is bad enough *now*. As *The Economist* sounded off: "The boom that created a new class of tycoon has also created its nemesis: a new, educated, urban, taxpaying middle class that is pushing for change. That is something corporate executives and elected leaders ignore at their peril."[8]

We say "Amen" and have created this book, in part, to awaken the working and middle class in the richest nation in the world to the realization that we do *not* have to play along with any version of the corporate market system. Rather, we should use the power of our vote (welcome President Trump) to demand federal tax code parity in order to return true competition to its key and essential place in the American capitalist system.

8

CHAPTER SIX

THE UNACCEPTABLE
NEW NORMAL

What does this New Normal look like, created by Wall Street's almost-absolute power? Here are a few facts and figures for you to consider.

Susan Heavey reported for Reuters on a recent study done by NYU and the University of California that revealed the difficulty of climbing the economic ladder in the United States today. Entitled "U.S. Economic Mobility Hampered by Growing Wealth Gap: Study," the article shared findings that demonstrated not only the dimmer prospects for low- and middle-class Americans but for their cities as well. The study of ninety-six metropolitan areas across the country, commissioned by the Pew Charitable Trusts, found cities far less economically mixed than they were just decades ago. Cities are increasingly segregated according to class, with enclaves of the wealthy walled off from the commoners. NYU sociology professor Patrick Sharkey summarized the findings succinctly: "There are more neighborhoods where poverty is more concentrated and wealth is more concentrated."

Not only do neighborhoods look different, but families' entire economic future can be affected. Low-income families in more divided cities take a full four generations to reach half the nation's mean income, for example, while in more-mixed urban zones, that number is cut to three generations. The most deeply divided cities include New York, Newark, Washington, and Los Angeles. The poorer areas, Sharkey said, not only have substandard housing in many cases, but they receive less school funding and have higher crime rates. "We should really be thinking about economic mobility at a more local level," he noted, adding, "It's a trend that makes us think that cities will become less of an engine for economic mobility if they keep trending toward a scenario where the rich live in separate communities from the poor."[31]

Statistical tables "relating to income, employment and production" at Whitehouse.gov unveil many disturbing numbers, such as:

- GDP contraction from double-digit growth in some years in the 1970s and 1980s to -2% (2008), -1.70/0 (2009)
- Median American income dropped nearly $1,500 between 1998 and 2009.
- The percentage of those below the poverty line growing from 10% to 11.1%.
- Weekly earnings for the average American have not stagnated; they've dipped in recent years. Social mobility in reverse: middle class went to working class and working class went to poor.

Consider these percentage changes in weekly earnings from the year 2000: -0.1, 1.2, 0, -0.5, -0.6, 1, 1, 1, 0, -1, 0, 2, 2, 1, 0.

In short, American workers have gained almost nothing in true buying power, and that is only for the average worker. What about the large number who have not even fared as well in weekly earnings increases as indicated above?[32]

Tyler Durden reported for the website Zerohedge.com that home ownership figures in recent years are even worse than previously thought. As he wrote, "An entire generation [the millennials] is locked out of purchasing a home due to over $1 trillion in student loans hanging over their heads. Every financial decision, an abysmal jobs market [for everyone but college-educated waiters and bartenders whose hiring is on a tear] forcing millions of Americans to rent instead of buy, has been duly documented here before." Durden went on to demonstrate how the previously reported homeownership rate was the lowest since 1965, but the calculation was adjusted according to a metric that was not entirely accurate. In fact, the rate was even lower than widely reported, a stunning 63.1%, the lowest since at least 1983. As Durden wrote, "The reality is that not only is the American Dream now completely over, but that the American Nightmare has never been worse."[3] An astonishing 110 million Americans are on welfare, as of the fourth quarter in 2012. That's more than one in three Americans, our New Normal. Here is part of the breakdown of that huge number:

- 51 million on food stamps
- 23 million on WIC
- 13 million with housing subsidies

To put the total in perspective, consider that 110 million is more than the combined populations of the United Kingdom and Ukraine. Or understand that there are more people on welfare than who work full-time, year round. That's unbelievable, but true.[34]

The labor force participation rate is also incredibly low, dipping to numbers not seen since the late '70s during the "malaise" under President Jimmy Carter. By the way, this is why you cannot always take unemployment percentages at face value. They build off a total of people who could potentially be in the workforce, people who are seeking jobs. So many millions of Americans have stopped trying to find employment that the numbers are altered. How many people are out of work, either by choice or by not looking? Try 92 million, or 37.3%, a percentage not seen since 1978.[35]

While some progress has been made on the unemployment rate in the past few years, the percentages are still far higher than in previous decades. The U6 unemployment rate, which includes "marginally attached workers and those working part time for economic reasons" hit an astonishing high of 17.1% in 2009-2010 but has dipped to 8.9% in 2017, a nice decrease but still a rate more than 50% higher than in the year 2000. Part of the New Normal is simply accepting double-digit U6 unemployment rates and rejoicing that they are not over 20%![36]

If we break down some of these dismal numbers by ethnic group, the news gets even more upsetting, a lot more, especially for young people. Part of what has happened is that adults desperate for work are doing jobs that teenagers used to do, such as delivering newspapers and flipping burgers. Consequently, teens are getting shut out of the labor market and failing to develop the type of work ethic that they can carry on when they work full-time as adults. An entire generation is not working because older people have pushed them out of the labor force. Here's a number that should shock you:

- 92% of African-American male teens in Chicago do not work, partly because the state of Illinois has 600,000 fewer jobs today than it did in 2000.

- Nationwide, 83% of our country's male teens aged sixteen to nineteen do not work.

The New Normal obviously does not see teen employment as important for the economy, character development, or enriching urban communities.[9] It's not bad enough that income disparity is worsening. A look at retirement savings will reveal that the disparity continues and even worsens when a person reaches senior status. When our economy shifted from pension plans supporting retired workers to their own savings keeping them afloat, the gap between rich and poor ripped open like cheap upholstery. As the Economic Policy Institute reported in a recent article, "The 401(k) revolution created a few big winners and many losers." The result is "retirement insecurity has worsened for most Americans as retirement wealth has become more unequal." In fact, the median household has *no* savings in retirement accounts, and even those that do have low balances in most cases. The institute's article on this topic noted that 401(k)'s were "an accident of history" and "Congress did not intend for them to replace traditional pensions as a primary retirement vehicle, and 401(k)'s are poorly designed for this role." Furthermore, participation in 401(k)'s and similar programs is on the decline as employees seek to hold on to more of their weekly paychecks. This phenomenon also means that the average worker, even if he or she does participate in a 401(k), is far more susceptible to recessions in the larger economy, as well as possible depressions. The article's conclusion paraphrased the bad news this way: "The trends… paint a picture of increasingly inadequate savings and retirement income… and growing disparities by income, race, ethnicity, education, and marital status, Even women, who by some measures appear to be nar-

---

9

rowing gaps with men, are ill-served by an inefficient retirement system that shifts risk onto workers, including the risk of outliving one's retirement savings."[38]

Speaking of 401(k)'s, one reason why they are not ideal instruments for retirement savings is the massive hidden fees that go along with them. Dailyfinance.com unearthed a recent study showing that the average worker who gives to such accounts can be quietly charged $155,000 over the course of a career.[39]

Fund managers grab these fees and the gap between the upper and middle classes continues to widen. Perhaps it's testament to our meek acceptance of the New Normal that we are not surprised whatsoever to hear that few people are saving well for retirement, and even those who do are charged tens of thousands of dollars in fees.

Many sites on the web highlight the relationship between a favorable tax code and the rich gobbling up wealth. Salon.com did an outstanding job summarizing this problem succinctly with its recent article entitled "10 Tax Dodges That Help the Rich Get Richer."[10] One memorable quote from that summary went this way: "Many of the most egregious tax avoidance scams are perfectly legal." To summarize the most prominent loopholes that have enabled the rich to grab an even bigger piece of the pie and keep the middle and working classes tamped down. What most of us would define as "income" in a common sense manner, the tax code does not. Here are the objectionable ways that the super-rich avoid paying taxes:

- Billionaires earn much of their money in carried interest and the appreciation of their stock, real estate, and other assets.

10

- Their salaries, if they have them, are negligible.
- Even when their income is more tangible in the form of capital gains, they pay a tax rate that is about half what the average working person does.

No wonder Congress has been trying to close this loophole since 2007, but for now, the lobbyists are winning the battle.

When seemingly generous wealthy people pour money into nonprofit organizations, sometimes it is indeed to benefit others, but in other instances, it can function strictly as a tax shelter for a donor and his and her heirs. The law does not require such organizations to spend their wealth or pay estate taxes and the like. The fascinating rush to give to these sorts of charities exhibited by a large group of financiers in recent years might be for a more sinister purpose unfortunately.

The ultra-rich are also able to claim an astonishing variety of "offsetting expenses" as they calculate their taxes. This could vary from skyboxes at professional sports events to fancy restaurants, from corporate jets to corporate chefs to corporate apartments—the types of perks that the 1% know all about but the rest of us can't even imagine—all tax-free. A clarifying simple example would be the average person's inability to deduct the expenses associated with the used car he or she drives to work while the Goldman Sachs banker who rides home in a corporate limo does so in the name of his company's business expenses. And it gets worse: many companies insist that CEOs use corporate jets for all trips, even vacations, so that all of it can be deducted as an offsetting expense. Even the breaks we regular Joes receive by contributing to IRAs, for instance, are sweeter for the more privileged among us. Certain types of pension plans such as those used by law firm partnerships, joint medical practices, and the like, allow contributions up to three times greater than the $17,500 maximum for the rest of us. Worse yet, a veritable army is working day and night to expand the tax breaks that these massive companies and their top employees enjoy. Nearly eighteen thousand plump, powdered, polished, and pinstriped professional lobbyists are continually pushing for more deductions to help the wealthy create more wealth and find even more ways to shelter their earned or inherited riches.[40]

Whatever your opinion on the validity of these shelters, loopholes, and credits, the obvious question that is rarely asked is: "Why are none of these major tax breaks and benefits designed to help middle-class working Americans? Have we become so jaded by the New Normal that we simply assume tax shelters apply only to wealthy?"

We would argue that the same breaks listed above need to be extended again to the middle- and upper-middle-class Americans who have typically driven the engine of investment and advancement in our country. It's time to restart the most powerful economic engine in the world—America's savvy businesspeople—who are ready and willing to invest in small businesses, if they can be assured that their risk will be reduced through reasonable tax codes. In short, people need to be considered as corporations too, not just the other way around.

The end result of the corporate market system / crony capitalism has not been the trickle-down effect that many have argued would occur over the several decades. Instead, it has created an investor monopoly that suffocates the dreams of the middle classes, thus choking the larger US economy. Have you also ever wondered why our economy has continued to sputter since tax laws have been revamped and wealth has become concentrated in the accounts of a few? That is no accident or coincidence. During the 1980s, Congress regulated the investment function and effectively terminated the free market system and created this corporate market system. This action planted the seed for our current situation—New Normal.

What's the answer? Not reducing or changing the corporate benefits of tax credits, loopholes, and shelters, but leveling the playing field of taxation for Main Street investors and changing the New Normal to the former American Dream, which has long offered equal opportunity for all. What needs to occur is that not only should corporations be treated as people, but also, people need to be treated as Wall Street corporations. If these corporations are not required to comply with Section 469 of the IRS code, then neither should the individual be discriminated against by applying the active-passive rules to them. It is high time to stop allowing Wall Street's monopoly dictate the New Normal and return true free market competition into capital investment, thereby creating an equal opportunity for all citizens to achieve the American Dream (Main Street investors versus Wall Street investors).

In the United States, we have always at least paid lip service to the importance of small businesses. If they are indeed the foundation of a healthy economy, then that makes small investors the very heartbeat of the American Dream. The reason for this is simple—the eliminating of investments in new Main Street businesses has produced the New Normal.

Thus, if we truly believe that small business is the backbone of our economy, then the investors with an exponential employment relationship should be encouraged and protected. Most investors in small businesses do not have billions to throw around, or even millions. Many give a man or a woman with a dream $50,000, for example, with the plan to recoup their capital and retain the investment for their retirement. In other words, they are solidly middle-class people in many cases.

Yet this bloodline to small business has been eliminated from the heart of the US economy by the 1986 Tax Simplification Act, which created the passive-activity regulations, a move that basically terminated the ability of Main Street investors from investing in businesses outside their employment discipline.

These passive-activity regulations do not apply to Wall Street investors, revealing a clear discrimination against the Main Street investor in favor of the corporate market system.

What happened very quickly was that Main Street investors stopped pouring money into small businesses, and the very act of investment quickly morphed into a privilege for only accredited investors (Wall Street). Again, we accept this reality so easily because we have been brainwashed into these Wall Street substitutes—i.e., 401(k) Roth IRA and alike.

In fact, restricting investment to only the Wall Street corporations violates the basic principles of capitalism and freedom. This policy has condemned our country to stagnation and has killed the individual's initiative to pursue the American Dream. Now, when someone wishes to invest, he or she can often only do so in a huge fund that decides which businesses will be allocated any capital resources. The power has dramatically shifted from the individual to the wealthy (i.e. Shark Tank).

When all's said and done, when all the facts and figures are reviewed and digested, the end result is the absolute exclusion of a large percentage of American citizens from the pursuit of the traditional dream. We cry out with the same spirit that democracy-loving American leaders drew on to challenge their communist enemies. Our cry echoes the same sentiment, "Tear down this Wall Street monopoly!" We call for the destruction of the status quo in order to build a new one. We need a level playing field, on which the American Dream is still alive and attainable for all. In fact, we will go one step further—if the huge corporations on Wall Street are not required to comply with section 469 of the IRS tax code, then neither should potential individual investors in the United States be hampered by application of this crippling regulation. We have never lived in a time where free market investing is as needed, and we need not be forced to accept this New Normal.

Repealing section 469, along with targeted initiatives (i.e. jobs credits and investment tax credits) to enable the middle class to invest locally would resurrect the American Dream. If we research the effects of the Liberty Zone [New York's 911 districts] we find that for five years, Section 469 was relaxed and the New York Liberty Zone had a quick recovery. The same can be said about the Gulf Zone which had a speedy recovery after hurricane Katrina.

At minimum, we should apply this program for a limited time, to our blighted inner cities, thereby extending hope to the hopeless with inner city capitalism.

Perhaps you've been overwhelmed by all of the numbers and graphs and references to legal cases as you've read over the pages of this book. Let's close with a look back 100 years to 1910-20 and we find the identical fate of inequality. Then, as now, 10% of the population consumed 55% of the income and controlled 80% of the wealth.

Not so surprising when a political system goes from a free market to a corporate market economy.

The process of adjusting the system back to a free market economy came with president Theodore Roosevelt's famous programs;

1. Square Deal
2. Trust {corporations} busting

All of which is sorely needed today,

1. Square Deal

a) Competition-as stated: Main Street vs. Wall Street repealing section 469 of the IRS code.{Passive vs. Active Rules}
b) Consumer Protection-we should protect the home buyer from predatory lending practices by repealing the Alternative Mortgage Parity Transaction Act and thereby allowing states to control home mortgage interest rates.

2. Trust Busting-when 50 Us corporations control 40% of our twenty trillion dollar economy, we should review these oligarchies for any anti-trust violations.

The New Normal Is Unacceptable

This book has offered myriad reasons why the American Dream has become so elusive for the very citizens that it used to motivate the lower and middle classes. After hours of research and discussion, however, we believe that one overlooked reason stands above many others as the trigger for the enormous wealth gap that we now have in America.

The business cycle has been materially altered over the past three to four decades with elimination of competition between Wall Street investors and Main Street investors. Repealing IRS Section 469 will repair our free market by returning competition, and creating millions of *Shark Tank*-like investment groups that will, in turn, produce inclusive economic growth. However, if we continue on this path of unfair free market restrictions, we, ultimately, will arrive at the door of a social democracy.

CHAPTER SEVEN

SUMMARY

The purpose of this thesis is to answer the question, why has the American Dream eluded so many of our median household income families, remembering that this group makes up 50% of our population or approximately one hundred sixty million individuals?

In a recent poll, for this segment of our population, it was revealed that over 50% of the respondents stated that they are not living the American Dream, and another 20% stated that the Dream is out of reach for them and their families.

When questioned as to why this condition has shattered their hopes, the overwhelming response is the unfair or the inequitable distribution of our annual income in the United States.

To verify this position, we reviewed the Government's publications and announcements, and currently identified that 10% of our population consumes 55% of our income, and the next 40% of our population consumes 30% of our income, and therefore our median household income families only have 15% of our income to share with 50% of the population. This seems inequitable and very concerning.

Based on this information, we decided to see how unfair we are, as compared to our global neighbors. When we reviewed the GINI CO-EFFICIENT which measures the amount of inequality for thirty six developed countries' income distributions, we were shocked to see that the U.S. currently ranks as the most unfair, unequitable, and disproportionate distributor of its annual income. How embarrassing, when countries with much fewer freedoms and opportunities than we have, can be fairer than we are in terms of income distribution.

It is no wonder, that in a recent poll of our children and grandchildren, the so-called Millennials, 50% of them favored a social democratic system over our free market system, and 10% suggested a communist system. This situation is far more than concerning or embarrassing; it is alarming.

This forces us to ask, how did we get here and how can we awaken from this nightmare? Or, in other words, what options do we have to solve this challenge?

If one were to trace the GINI CO-EFFICIENT back to 1901-1910, one will note, that for these years, the U.S.'s unfair income distribution was 10% of the population consuming 60% of our annual income, which is somewhat higher than our current situation of 55%. However, during this time we were fortunate to have a President who was both progressive and active in this regard, President Theodore Roosevelt, who in his effort to avoid a nationwide coal miners strike, became directly aware of the social and economic injustices cast upon the miners and their families, and did something about it.

To correct this injustice, President Roosevelt and his Administration developed a program called the "Square Deal," with a motto that "No one individual or business or organization should have an unfair advantage over the other."

To this end, the Roosevelt Administration structured a plan to level the playing field of fairness in our economy with the three C's for calibrating the relationship between:

1. Corporate-labors accord with capital.
2. Consumer-capitals accord for consumer protection.
3. Conservation-governments accord with capital for natural and human resources allocation.

Thereafter, with various legislative enforcement and executive orders, and the tightening of regulations, aimed at obtaining an equilibrium point of fairness, in each of the three C's, Theodore Roosevelt, and his Administration, changed the trajectory of the GINI CO-EFFICIENT to a downward slope. This downward slope continued until the 1980's and cut our inequity for income distribution by 50%, with the 10% of our population consuming only 30% of our annual income.

However, since the 1980's there have been various points of fairness which have been fragmented, confused, and disrupted, as noted in our previous chapters, through taxation, legislation, regulations, and executive order. These forces have impacted GINI CO-EFFICIENT to an upward slope, to where we are today, at an absolute point of inequality.

To awaken from this nightmare, and in order to preempt a radical shift to a hardcore socialist economy, we need to apply a similar plan to balance the three C's, with a new Square Deal. In other words, we need to better calibrate the fairness relationship of the corporations with labor, consumer, and government.

As a suggestion for greater fairness:

1. Corporate and labor relationship, ie; minimum wage should be indexed to CPI.
2. Corporate and consumer fairness, ie; corporate debt and student debt, should be treated equally in bankruptcy.
3. Corporate and government/equal treatment for business and government. If we had an Internet Tax

Freedom Act for twenty years, then we should have an Inner-City Tax Freedom Act for the next twenty years.

As stated in our book, it is necessary to implement various changes throughout our economy, with a renewed attitude toward both social and economic justice, and with a paradigm shift in our thinking for fairness. With a Square Deal, we will revive the American Dream and prevent a predictable and preventable nightmare.

References

Reference 1: http://www.alternet.org/economy/7-facts-show-american-d rea m-dead.

Reference 2: http://monev.usnews.com/monev/personal-finance/articles/2012f09/25/is-the-american-dream-dead. Updated

Reference 4: http:/hvwvw.pewtrusts.orq/en/research-and-analysis,/reports/0001101101 'moving-on-up.

Reference 5: http://www.washinqtonpost.com/wp-srv/special/national/economic-mobility-map/.

Reference 6: http://www.infowars.com/84-statistics-that-prove-the-decline-of-the-middIe-class-is-real-and-that-it-is-get-tinq-worse/. Updated

Reference 7: http://wwvv.washingtonpost.com/business/economy/poverty-was-flat-in-2011-percentage-without-health-insurance-fell/2012109112/0e04632c-fc29-11 el -8adc-499 661afe377 storv.html. Updated

Reference 8: http://www.epi.org/publication/the sad but true story of wages in america/.

Reference 9: https://www.youtube.com/watch?v=QPKKQ niinsM.

Reference 10: http://www.motherjones.com/politics/2011/02/ income-inequali!y-in-america-chart-graph.

Reference 11: http://thinkproqress.org/economy/2012/11 Il 6/1204871 /why-income-inegualitv-.

Reference 12: http:/{economistsview.typepad.corn/economists-view!2014/12/why-americas-middle-class-is-lost. Html.

Reference 13: http://www.bloomberg.com/bw/articles/2014-05-15/wny-americas-middle-class-housing-crunch-is-here-to-stay.

Reference 14: http://www.housingwire.com/articles/32079-trulia-home-affordability-siips-for-middle-class.

Reference 15: http://www.dailyfinance.com/2014/11 Il 4/middle-class-cant-buv-homes-in-most-big-cities/.

Reference 16: http://www.forecast-chart.com/graph-housing-starts.html.

Reference 17: http:/lwv.w.'.prb.org/Publications/Articles/2013/ us-owners-re nters-housing. aspx (Thursday, June 30, 2016 AOL: Turnberryr, page 2 of 2). Updated

Reference 18: http://wmv.usatodav.com/storv/money/business/2014/05/13/housing: affordabilib'.-worsens/9034185/.

Reference 19: http•.!lwww.washingtonpost.com/blogs/wonk blog/WQ/2013109/06/the-incredible-shrinking-labor-force-aqain/.

Reference 20: http://www.cbsnews.com/news/disability-usa/.

Reference 21: http://www.nytimes.com/2014/06/07/U pshot/good-n rent-we-ha ppier.

Reference 22: http://www.cepr.net/index.php/bloqs/beat-the-press/the-question-on-people-leaving-the-labor-force-is-ear-olds-not-61- ear-olds.

Reference 23: http://www.washinqtonpost.com/business/on-small-business/more-businesses-are-closinq-than-startinq-can-conqress-help-turn-that-around/2014/09/17/06576cb8-385a-1 le4-8601-97ba88884ffd story.html.

Reference 2:4 http : //www.breitbart.com/big-government/2015/01 / 14/economic-death-spiral-more-american-busi-nesses-dvinq-than-starting/.

Reference 25: h ://vrww.bls. ov/bdm/entre reneurshi lentre reneurshi .htm.

Reference 26: https://www.fas.orq/sqp/crs/misc/RL33069.pdf.

Reference 27: http://wrvvw.theatlantic.com/politics/arChive/2012/07 e-supreme-court-still-thinks-corpprations-are-pe0 Dle/25ggg5/.

Reference 28: htto://www.straightdope.com/columns/read/2469/ how-can-a-corpqration-be-legally-considered-a-person.

Reference 29: http://wwrw.motheriones.com/environment/ 2011 Il O/food-industry-monopoly-occupy-wail-street.

Reference 30: CAPITALISM http:/jwww.economist.com/news/ leaders/21598gg6-political-connections-have-made-ma-ny-people-hugely-rich-recent-years-crony-capitalism-may (Thursday, June 30, 2016 AOL: Turnberryr

Page I of I).

Reference 31: http://mvw.huffingtonpost.com/2013/12/04/ economic-mobility-usa n 4386711. Updated

Reference 32: https:Æwww.whitehouse.qov/sites/defauWfiles/ microsites/2011 erp appendixB.Ddf.

Reference 33: http://www.zerohedge.com/news/2015-03-09/ american-nightmare-shocker-real-us-homeownership-rate-has-never-been-lower.

Reference 34: newsartcan-http://wvav.cnsnews.com/commen-tarv/terence-p-ieffreW354-percent-109631000-welfare.

Reference 35: record-g26-miNion-ameriqans-not-lab0[4Q.

Reference 36: http://portalseven.com/emnlovment/unemplov-ment rate u6.isp.

Reference 37: http://vw.vw.mvfoxchicaqo.com/story/244866 94/new-study-finds-92-percent-0f-african-americao-male-teens-are-unemp'oyad.

Reference 38: httm//www_epi_ora/publiqation/retirement-ineauality-chartbook/.

Reference 39: http://www.dailyfinance.com/2012/06/05/hidden-401k-fees-retirement-plan-ripoff/.

Reference 40: http://wwy..salon.com/2013/04/12/10 tax dod-qes gnat help the rich qe! richer partner.

https://wm.voutube.com/watch?v=QPKKQniinsM.

Reference 41: http://www.huffinqtonpost/2011/12/12small-business-loans n 1121955.html (retrieved 5/5/2015).

About the Author

Raymond J. Parello grew up in Pittsburgh, Pennsylvania and attended the University of Pittsburgh where he received a Bachelor of Science Degree and then went on to get his Masters Degree from Duquesne University. He also became a member of Pennsylvania Institute of Certified Public Accountants.

He served his country during the Vietnam War in the United States Airforce and started his career at Price-Waterhouse.

He has spent the last forty years as Financial Director for a real estate holding company developing and managing malls, hotels, condominiums, office buildings, and country clubs.

He lives in Miami, Florida with his wife Ellie.

revivingthedream@aol.com

CPSIA information can be obtained
at www.ICGtesting.com
Printed in the USA
LVHW030240311018
595214LV00005B/375/P